W9-API-907

CLASSIC WARPLANES

McDONNELL DOUGLAS AH-64 APACHE

Bob Munro

GALLERY BOOKS

An Imprint of W. H. Smith Publishers Inc.
112 Madison Avenue
New York City 10016

A SALAMANDER BOOK

©Salamander Books Ltd. 1991
129-137 York Way,
London N7 9LG,
United Kingdom.

ISBN 0-8317-1405-0

This edition published in 1991 by Gallery
Books, an imprint of W.H. Smith
Publishers, Inc., 112 Madison Avenue,
New York, New York 10016.

Gallery Books are available for bulk
purchase for sales promotions and
premium use. For details, write or
telephone the Manager of Special Sales,
W.H. Smith Publishers, Inc., 112
Madison Avenue, New York, New York
10016. (212) 532-660.

All correspondence concerning the
content of this volume should be
addressed to Salamander Books Ltd.

This book may not be sold outside the
United States of America or Canada.

CREDITS

Editor: Peter Hall
Designers: Oxprint Ltd., England
Color Artwork: ©Salamander Books
Ltd., England
Three-view and cutaway drawings:
©Pilot Press, England
Filmset by: The Old Mill, England
Color separation by Graham Curtis
Repro, England
Printed in Belgium by Proost International
Book Production, Turnhout

AUTHOR

BOB MUNRO'S working life has been entirely associated with military subjects
and the world of publishing, starting in 1981 with work on a series of aviation-
oriented publications, and including writing and photography for a variety of articles.
A keen aviation enthusiast with a particular interest in the concept of the attack
helicopter and its operational deployment, he continues to pursue a career in the
world of military publishing.

CONTENTS

HISTORY tells us that the origins of the helicopter date back to the 12th Century, when the first example of such a machine was flown as a string-pulled toy; yet it is only in the 20th Century that the concept of rotary-winged flight has, quite literally, taken off. The history of helicopters equipped for military purposes is even more recent, and it is all too easy in this age of hi-tech "tank busters", as represented by the subject of this book, to lose sight of the fact that the initial use of militarized helicopters, albeit somewhat rudimentary designs, ocurred less than 50 years ago, during the Second World War.

As was the case in several other areas of aviation at that time, German designers, most notably Anton Flettner and Heinrich Focke, led the way. The German Navy in particular followed their work with interest, and by the mid-1940s small numbers of the Flettner Fl 282 Kolibri (*Humming Bird*) and the Focke-Achgelis Fa 330 Bachstelze (*Water Wagtail*) were in use on convoy protection and target location duties from Navy ships and submarines respectively.

Both designs were intended first and foremost as observation platforms and the nearest either came to sporting any form of armament was a telephone, as used by the pilot of the Fa 330 to communicate his observations from on high to the commander of his U-boat "home", some 400ft (122m) below on the ocean surface.

Arming helicopters was all but inevitable, however, and another of the Focke designs, the much larger and more versatile Fa 223 Drache (*Kite*), was soon carrying a single MG 15 machine-gun and two 551lb (250kg) bombs for anti-submarine operations.

Above: Though quite ungainly in appearance, the Flettner Fl 282 was both manoeuvrable and stable. Some 20 examples were used on convoy protection duties.

Below: Lighter and simpler than the Fl 282, the Fa 330 single-seat, unpowered observation kite was "flown" from German U-Boats on target location tasks.

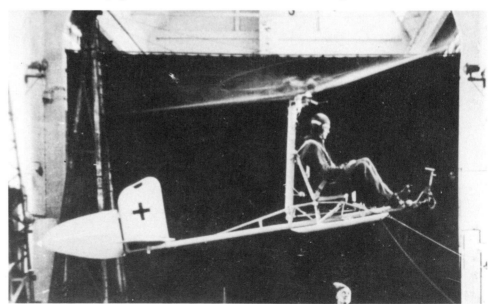

powerful designs capable of lifting ever greater payloads of both men and their machinery.

As the 1940s gave way to the 1950s, however, the United States found itself involved in another war, this time on the Korean Peninsula. The Korean War marked the first large-scale use of helicopters for military tasks; but the vast majority were models produced by the likes of Bell and Sikorsky for use as transports, carrying fresh troops and equipment into the battle zone, and flying the wounded out on casualty evacuation (casevac) missions. Small numbers of such helicopters were armed, but the addition of one or two machine-guns, or maybe a bazooka-type rocket pack grafted onto the airframe, was modest at best and very much an afterthought.

Nevertheless, progress was being made, and lessons learnt during the Korean War were soon being put to good use by the Army back in the United States. The result was a series of test and evaluation programmes conducted during the mid-1950s, in which helicopters such as the Bell H-13 Sioux and Hiller H-23 Raven, as well

Above: Used for evaluation in a number of roles, the distinctive Fa 223 Drache (*Kite*) was also the world's first helicopter to carry onboard armament.

Below: Synonymous with casualty evacuation (casevac) during the Korean War, the Bell H-13 Sioux typified the non-aggressive use of early post-war helicopters.

PROGRESS SLOWS

Though it promised much, further development of this and other German militarized helicopters was curtailed by the prosecution of the Second World War and the eventual Allied victory. The United States had been making steady progress in the field of helicopter design, primarily as a result of the work of Igor Sikorsky, but there was seemingly a lack of momentum in the immediate post-war years to fully exploit the undoubted potential of armed helicopters.

Instead, the emphasis was on developing helicopters primarily for transport roles, with manufacturers making the most of technological advances to produce larger and more

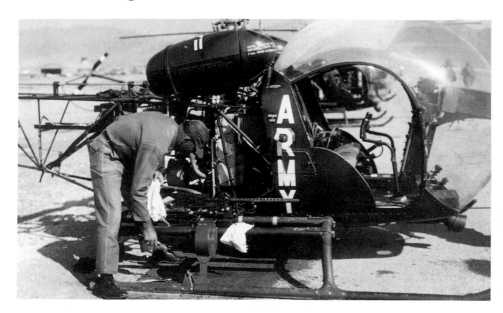

Above: Primed for armed combat tests thanks to a pair of .30in (7.62mm) guns and folding-fin aerial rockets, this US Army H-13 packed quite a "punch".

as larger types such as the Sikorsky H-19 Chickasaw and the Piasecki H-21 Shawnee, were fitted with a variety of machine-guns, gun pods and rocket packs to establish their effectiveness as weapons platforms.

On the whole, the results of such tests were encouraging; and the concept of the well-armed helicopter received a further boost with the adoption by the US Army of a new operational philosophy based on the concept of "air mobility", whereby a heliborne mobile fighting force could be deployed quickly on and around the battlefield. These "air cavalry" helicopters would be escorted by a "flying artillery" force of helicopters armed to provide cover firepower.

To an extent, such an operational concept had already been evaluated under combat conditions by the French Army when it attempted to quell a rebel uprising in Algeria. The rough, often inaccessible North African terrain led to a heavy reliance on troop-carrying helicopter "gunships" armed with cannon and machine-guns to carry out counter-insurgency (COIN) operations.

The US Army took note of the French Army's experience with its "gunships"; but it soon found itself learning first-hand how such weapons platforms could best be employed. Ironically, France's inability to crush an uprising in Indo-China had set in motion a chain of events which, in the early-1960s, were set to embroil the United States in a long, drawn-out and bloody conflict. For Indo-China, read Vietnam.

ENTER THE "HUEY"

The US Army's early experience in the Vietnam War was to have a crucial bearing on the development of the attack helicopter. The "air mobile" concept was by now an intrinsic part of the Army's operational doctrine, helped in no small measure by the acquisition and operation of one particular helicopter type.

The Bell Model 204 had first flown in late 1956, and the US Army soon

Above: Larger transport types, like this H-21 Shawnee, were also armed by the US Army for test and evaluation purposes.

realized that here was the ideal transport helicopter with which it could make the concept of an "air mobile" force an operational reality. In military guise, the Model 204 was officially known as the HU-1, (the letters denoting its "Helicopter Utility" role), but to one and all it was simply the "Huey", even when its designation was changed to UH-1.

In a variety of guises, the ubiquitous "Huey" was to become synonymous with US operations in Vietnam, and these included its use as

Above: The Vietnam War saw the arrival of the armed helicopter in its truest sense, with the door-mounted M-50 machine-gun a stalwart of fire cover tasks.

Above: For a relatively small and light helicopter, the UH-1 could lift a quite prodigious weapons load, such as this "twin pack" of TOW missiles.

the "Slicks" (unarmed, troop-carrying UH-1s)), laying down a screen of defensive fire as the latter made their way in and out of the designated combat landing zones.

Above: Framed by the canopy and sighting unit, rockets fired by a well-armed UH-1 "Hog" at Viet Cong emplacements register their arrival in the dense jungle.

Above: Forever associated with US involvement in the Vietnam War, the ever-dependable UH-1 "Huey" was first and foremost a transport for the "grunts".

a "gunship". Indeed, its arrival led directly to the formation of the US Army's first armed helicopter unit, officially known as the Utility Tactical Transport Helicopter Company (UTTHC), which was soon despatched to South-East Asia with UH-1As to evaluate further the armed helicopter operational concept.

The results soon led to the deployment of many more armed "Hueys", carrying a variety of weapons ranging from the door-mounted M-60 .30in (7.62mm) machine-gun to a nose-mounted M-5 1.58in (40mm) grenade-launcher, and from packs of 2.75in (70mm) rockets to Minigun pods and a Mortar Air Delivery System. These armed "Hogs" would ride shotgun for

MEETING THE NEED

But as good as these armed "Hueys" proved to be, the truth was that such machines were, once again, primarily adaptations of a helicopter originally designed to operate in the utility role. As the Vietnam War progressed, it became increasingly clear that the US Army needed a dedicated "gunship"; a helicopter designed from the outset to specialize in the conduct of close air support operations.

Accordingly, in mid-1963, the Army formalized its operational requirement in its Fire Support Aerial System (FSAS) project. The title was soon changed to the Advanced Aerial Fire Support System (AAFSS) and a Request for Proposals released to the aerospace industry. Paper studies led to the selection of a Lockheed design as winner, with funding being provided for the construction of no less than 10 pre-production examples of what

Roles and Requirements

Above: A seemingly formidable addition to the world of the ''gunship'', the Lockheed AH-56 Cheyenne never quite lived up to its undoubted potential.

was to be known as the AH-56A Cheyenne: the world's first dedicated attack helicopter.

The Cheyenne was very much an investment in the future, the Army being under no illusions that it would take some considerable time to hone Lockheed's design into a front-line fighting machine. At the same time, the Vietnam War was escalating and there was a pressing need for an interim armed helicopter to fill the gap between the existing ''Hueys'' and the arrival of the Cheyenne.

Fortunately for the Army, Bell, makers of the UH-1, had not been resting on its laurels. Aware for some time that what the Army needed was a dedicated attack helicopter, a company-funded programme led to what was known as the Model 207 Sioux Scout. Based on a radically altered Model 47 Sioux, it featured a much narrower fuselage, with tandem seating for the co-pilot/gunner (front) and the pilot (rear) replacing the standard side-by-side arrangement in transport helicopter designs.

Beneath the nose was an Emerson Tactical Armament Turret (TAT) housing a pair of .30in (7.62mm) machine-guns, and stub wings were fitted to enable heavier ordnance to be carried. Such features were, coincidentally, to appear on the AH-56A Cheyenne in due course.

The Sioux Scout took to the air for the first time in July 1963, and subsequent testing of this quite radical machine proved to be highly encouraging. Consequently, Bell took the UH-1's proven main rotor and engine and mated them with the fundamental elements of the Model 207. The result was a sleek and purposeful machine, impressively armed and with a fuselage cross-section of just 38in (9.65cm), which took to the air for the first time in September 1965. Just over seven months later, the US Army placed an order for 110 production examples; a figure that would rise to over 1,800 over the next two years.

''A'' FOR ATTACK

Known to Bell as the Model 209, the new machine bore the military designation AH-1G, the two-letter prefix identifying its ''Attack Helicopter'' role. It was also given a name, the first part of which reflected its descendancy from the UH-1, while the second part highlighted its ability to strike in anger with its own type of venom. The newest addition to the Army's airborne inventory, and its first dedicated attack helicopter, was christened the HueyCobra.

Soon the HueyCobra was in action in Vietnam, proving itself a highly

Below: In complete contrast to the Cheyenne, Bell's Model 207 Sioux Scout was a simple, no-nonsense design, and the right machine at the right time.

Above: From the Bell Model 207 emerged the AH-1 HueyCobra; a slender yet spirited combatant and the US Army's first truly dedicated attack helicopter.

capable attack helicopter in the process. Its success can be gauged by the fact that several versions of the AH-1 are still in widespread front-line service with the US Army and Marine Corps, as well as several export customers around the world, some 25 years after its first flight.

The same cannot be said for the Lockheed AH-56A Cheyenne, however. Though it promised much, this highly advanced helicopter was burdened with fundamental design problems which would have taken far too much time, effort and money to iron out. The Army did get as far as ordering a batch of 375 production examples, but such faith was ultimately misguided and the Cheyenne development programme was cancelled in August 1972.

That cancellation of the Cheyenne had left the Army's armed helicopter procurement programme in a state of limbo was clear for all to see, and both Bell and Sikorsky were quick to offer their own solutions. The Army, however, went back to the drawing

board, assembling what was to be known officially as the Advanced Attack Helicopter (AAH) Task Force to ascertain and clarify its future AAH requirements.

Not surprisingly, the Army's attack helicopter operations during the Vietnam War were studied in detail; but so were the experiences of the various adversaries in the Arab-Israeli conflicts, as well as the nature of the

threat posed to the West by the massive build-up of Warsaw Pact armour forces in Eastern Europe.

The result was a Request For Proposals (RFP) issued to the US

Below: Just how slender the AH-1 is in comparison to its progenitor, the UH-1, can clearly be seen in this Bell "family photograph" of US Marine Corps machines.

Roles and Requirements

aerospace industry in November 1972 which called for a state-of-the-art integrated helicopter weapons system tailored for anti-armour operations. Contenders would have to meet a series of stringent operational requirements for what was to be, in effect, a "tank buster" able to seek out, identify and "kill" armoured targets by day or night and in bad weather.

Despite such strict parameters, five companies (Bell, Boeing-Vertol, Hughes, Lockheed and Sikorsky) responded to the RFP; but the list of contenders to receive funding for Phase I of the AAH programme was soon reduced to just the Bell and Hughes entries by an Army Source Selection Evaluation Board.

Accordingly, $44.7 million and $70.3 million in engineering development contracts was awarded to Bell and Hughes respectively to cover the construction of one ground test vehicle

Below: The future of the attack helicopter takes shape in the form of the Hughes AH-64 full-scale mock-up, complete with quad TOW missile launchers and rocket pods.

(GTV), one static test vehicle (STV) and two flying prototypes of each design. In addition, Hughes would develop its XM230 Chain Gun, this separate programme accounting for the much larger financial award.

Both designs were to be twin-engined, relying for their power on the General Electric T700-GE-700 turboshaft engine. Having selected the winning airframe as a result of Phase I testing and evaluation, Phase II of the programme would comprise a full-scale engineering development programme in which the various mission systems and subsystems would be integrated and tested.

FIRST FLIGHTS

Bell's proposal, known in-house as the Model 409, received the Army designation YAH-63A; whilst the Hughes Model 77 became the YAH-64A. Both designs were to suffer early teething troubles which pushed the AAH programme back some six months, the Bell GTV being the first to come to life, with rotors turning on 19 April 1975. Just over two months later, on 22 June, and exactly

two years after the initial contracts had been awarded, Air Vehicle 01, (AV-01) the Hughes GTV, made its first ground-based engine run.

First to fly was the YAH-64A, the first prototype (AV-02) making a successful 38-minute maiden flight from Palomar Municipal Airport (MAP), California, on 30 September 1975. The very next day, Bell's first YAH-63A took to the skies above Arlington MAP, Texas, on a 24-minute first flight. Soon, the second prototypes of each design were up and running, with first flights for the Hughes and Bell designs on 22 November 1975 and 21 December 1975 respectively.

At first glance, the rival designs appeared to share several common features, such as tandem cockpits, twin engines and an undernose gun/aiming system location. But closer inspection revealed some very different design philosophies at work.

The YAH-63A was based on Bell's Model 309 KingCobra (the company's unsuccessful bid to fill the gap left by cancellation of the AH-56A Cheyenne), which was itself an outgrowth of the successful AH-1 HueyCobra. Unlike the AH-1, the YAH-63A's

Above: A close study of Bell's YAH-63A highlights distinct similairites with the earlier AH-1 HueyCobra, particularly in the fuselage lines and the flat-plate canopy glazing.

tandem cockpit arrangement placed the pilot in front and the co-pilot/gunner (CPG) behind; the company arguing that future anti-armour operations would be conducted at extremely low altitude, thus making an enhanced field-of-vision for the pilot an absolute necessity if he was to fly effectively. The CPG, however, would rely much more on head-down displays for target acquisition, thus rendering the need for a good field-of-view (i.e. from the front cockpit) all but obsolete.

DESIGN DIFFERENCES

The Bell proposal also featured a two-bladed main rotor, this being turned by power from the two T700 turboshafts, each of which was housed in blended, shoulder-mounted cowlings on the low-drag fuselage. A tricycle landing gear was fitted, and a 30mm, three-barrel XM188 gun was located immediately under the nose, with the sighting system for this weapon located further aft.

In contrast, the YAH-64A adopted a CPG/front and pilot/rear crew configuration, as featured in Bell's AH-1. A four-bladed main rotor was fitted, with the engines housed in separate boxes which stood proud of the upper mid-fuselage. A more conventional "taildragger" landing gear configuration was adopted, although the main units were swept back sharply. As with the crew arrangement, the undernose positioning of the XM230 Chain Gun and the weapon sighting system was the reverse of that adopted on the two Bell YAH-63A prototypes.

Throughout the first half of 1976, both Bell and Hughes put their respective designs through a series of exhaustive tests. The second half of 1976 was given over to Army testing and evaluation of the prototype machines at Edwards Air Force Base (AFB), California. Unfortunately for Bell, the first YAH-63A crashed just days before it was due to be shipped to Edwards for the start of the Phase I 90-hour fly-off, forcing the company to quickly bring its GTV up to full flight-test standard.

But the company's valiant efforts were in vain: on 10 December 1976, after an in-depth analysis of all aspects of the competing programmes, the Hughes YAH-64A was declared the winner of the Army's AAH programme. The company was duly awarded $317 million for the construction of three more prototypes, and a further $390 million to finance work on the Phase II subsystem engineering development programme.

Below: Having triumphed over the challenge from Bell, Hughes set about developing the Hellfire-equipped YAH-64 into a lean, mean, fighting machine.

COMMENCING in January 1977, Phase II of the US Army's AAH programme was to last 56 months and involve the two existing YAH-64A prototypes (AV-02/-03), as well as a trio of pre-production AH-64As (AV-04/-05/-06), the construction of which was funded as part of the programme. In short, the aim of Phase II was to integrate all relevant mission equipment and subsystems with the airframe itself, and to then thoroughly test the overall "package". The entire system would then be further tested by the Army under operational conditions as part of its Operational Test II (OT-II) evaluation. On the basis of the results of such tests would rest a decision regarding the future direction of the entire programme.

Initially, both AV-02 and -03 undertook Phase II test flights; but such activity soon revealed several aspects of the design for which modification was a necessity if the design was to prove a success. Accordingly, both helicopters

Below: Initial attempts to cure nap-of-the-earth handling woes were centred around turning the T-tail through 180deg and adding vertical endplates.

were grounded in May 1978 to receive what were known as Modification 1 (Mod 1) changes. Some six months later, the reconfigured AV-02 took to the air once again. Its stablemate stayed in the shop for another month while it received further alterations known, not surprisingly, as Modification 2 (Mod 2) changes.

Suitably refined, both prototypes returned to Phase II duties. For AV-02,

Above: One of the first company photographs of AV-02 and AV-03 in flight. At this stage, both sported the original T-tail and chin-mounted sensor turret.

MODIFICATIONS
Mod 1
1) Length of rotor mast increased by 6in (15cm)
2) Tail rotor diameter increased by 3in (7.5cm)
3) Swept tips added to main rotor blades
4) "Black Hole" IR-suppressor exhaust nozzles fitted to both engines
5) Straight leading-edge/tapered trailing-edge configuration adopted for T-tail
Mod 2
1) Replacement of flat-plate canopy glazing with single-curvature, low-glint panels
2) Expanded capacity in forward avionics bays
3) Fitment of electrical wiring and equipment to test onboard mission subsystems

the next major role was to act as a weapons platform during a series of test firings of Rockwell's Hellfire anti-armour missile subsystem. These were conducted at Marine Corps Air Station (MCAS) Camp Pendleton, California, and five such missiles had been fired successfully by May 1979. Testing then switched to Hughes' AAH Flight Test Center at Castle Dome Heliport, within the Yuma Proving Grounds in Arizona.

Here, both helicopters were fitted out with the rival designs of possibly the two most important subsystems of all. Known in full as the Target Acquisition and Designation Sight and the Pilot's Night Vision Sensor (TADS/PNVS), these nose-mounted sensors would form a crucial part of the helicopter's armoury. The competing designs were supplied by Martin Marietta and Northrop, and their respective sensor suites were duly loaded into AV-02 and AV-03 to evaluate their performance during a further series of missile shoots commencing in October 1979.

That same month, AV-04, the first of the three pre-production AH-64As, conducted a successful maiden flight. Its debut was significant, for the

Below: As OT-II testing continued, so the rival TADS/PNVS sensor suites from Martin Marietta (left) and Northrop (right) became the subject of a thorough evaluation.

machine incorporated a major change in tailplane configuration.

Test flying of the prototypes had revealed the helicopter to have poor low-level handling qualities, with a marked tendency to pitch upwards while flying "low-and-slow". For the CPG in the front cockpit, this nose-high attitude severely degraded his forward visibility — exactly what he didn't need if he was to employ the weapons systems effectively. For the pilot in the back seat, maintaining effective control of a somewhat unstable helicopter at such marginal altitudes resulted in a significant rise in his overall workload.

"TWEAKING" THE TAIL

The answer, as applied to AV-04, was the abandonment of the fixed T-tail in favour of an all-moving "stabilator" mounted at the base of

Above: Configured with the low-set horizontal stabilator, seen here at maximum deflection, the fourth YAH-64 (AV-04) was used for proof-of-concept evaluation.

the vertical fin. In addition, the height of the fin was increased by 3in (7.62cm) and the tail rotor assembly was repositioned 2ft 6in (76cm) higher on the fin. Subsequent "tweaking" resulted in a final configuration (first fitted to AV-06) incorporating the changes noted, as well as featuring a tail rotor diameter increased by 10in (25.4cm) and a "stabilator" slightly reduced in overall size.

Slowly but surely, a formidable fighting machine was taking shape. But tragedy was not far away. On 28 November 1980, AV-04 was involved in a mid-air collision with a North American T-28D Trojan photo-ship, while conducting what should have

A Winner Takes Shape

Above: Holding formation for the camera, AV-04 and -06 display the low-set stabilator, while AV-05 (centre) is devoid of any such horizontal unit.

been a routine test flight. Both aircraft were destroyed, and three of the four crew, including test pilot's James Grouix and John Ludwig aboard AV-04, were killed.

TESTING, TESTING

Convened at Hunter-Liggett Military Reservation, California, on 1 June 1981, the OT-II tests were conducted under the auspices of the Army's Combat Development Experimentation Command (CDEC). Using air and ground crews from the 7th Aviation Battalion/7th Infantry Division, the three-month programme tested the three pre-production AH-64As under realistic front-line combat scenarios, with much emphasis on "hands on" experience for the personnel who, assuming the helicopter went into full-scale production, might one day find themselves operating the AH-64A in combat.

The chances of that happening took a major step forward with a positive CDEC OT-II final report. The

Above: Of particular note in this view of AV-04 is the completely revised nose configuration, now dominated by the barrel-shaped unit housing the night systems sensor and TADS scanner.

report's recommendations, along with all aspects of the AAH programme, were then reviewed by the Army's Operational Test and Evaluation Agency. On the basis of its recommendations, the Defense Systems Acquisitions Review Council (DSARC) took the final decision regarding the future of the entire project.

Hughes, meanwhile, took the bold step of announcing in July 1981 its intention to build a brand new manufac-

turing facility specifically tailored to meet the needs of large-scale AH-64A production. At the very least, the decision — made before any final pronouncement from the DSARC in favour of full-scale production — served to underline the company's confidence in its product.

The site chosen for the new plant was located at Mesa, just outside Phoenix, Arizona. Whatever the business and economic reasons that influenced the choice of Mesa, its location seemed wholly appropriate from a historical perspective as well. In days gone by, the land that now forms the state of Arizona was the domain of a tribe of Native Americans whose fighting prowess and exploits in battle have become the stuff of legend. Proud and fearsome, their tribal name lent itself as the ideal monicker for the new armed warrior: APACHE.

Work on the five-building plant, spread out over some 576,000sq ft (53,517m²), began on 5 March 1982. With seemingly impeccable timing, the DSARC announced its final decision regarding AH-64A production just three weeks later: Hughes was authorized to start work on a batch of 11 full-scale production machines. Fittingly, the world's most advanced helicopter was to be built in the what Hughes proudly claimed would be the world's most advanced helicopter manufacturing plant.

All was not well, however, when it came to production costs. The original requirement had envisaged an initial production block of 14 Apaches being procured for $365 million. In reality, the batch was reduced by three machines — but funding rose to $444.4 million. The world's most advanced fighting helicopter was now by far the most expensive helicopter ever built, with a procurement unit cost (the flyaway unit cost plus the cost of all associated ground support) of over $10 million.

FIGHTING FOR FUNDS

Despite much heated discussion on Capitol Hill concerning the escalating costs of the Apache programme, and a refusal (albeit temporary) on the part of the politicians to authorize funding for a further 48 machines, the US Army held its ground. Hughes, meanwhile, started preparatory work in leased premises in the Phoenix area on Apache equipment. By March 1983, however, just one year after ground on the new site had been broken, work on the Mesa assembly facility had progressed sufficiently to allow work to be transferred there from the leased workspace units.

Once again, the timing was just right; at the Teledyne Ryan Aeronautical manufacturing plant in San Diego, California, work was being completed on the first production Apache fuselage. On Friday, 25 March, the fuselage, secured in a tractor-trailer unit known as an Aircraft Transportation Assembly Fixture (ATAF), began its journey to Mesa. On Monday, 28 March, the unit was installed on the assembly line at Mesa, and Hughes employees set to work on assembling Production Vehicle 01 (PV-01). Their work (at least at the initial Assembly Stations) was aided by the ATAF: acting as a giant cradle for the fuselage assembly, it could be raised some six feet (1.83m) and rotated

through 90deg to facilitate installation work on the line.

As work on PV-01 progressed in the following months, so work on the Mesa facility itself continued. Indeed, work on PV-01 at Mesa began some four months prior to completion of the Assembly and Flight Test Center. Despite this dual construction effort, work on PV-01 progressed smoothly, and on 30 September 1983, just over six months after work began at

Below: The comprehensive flight test programme included a series of icing trials, conducted over Minnesota during 1983. Icing on the airframe is indicated by the yellow discolouring.

A Winner Takes Shape

Above: Amid due ceremony, and with an Apache warrior very much in evidence, PV-01, the first production AH-64A Apache, was rolled out at Mesa on 30 September 1983.

Assembly Station 1 and two months ahead of schedule, the first full-scale production AH-64A Apache, flanked by an Apache warrior astride a gleaming white steed, was rolled out amid due pomp and ceremony.

For everyone concerned with the project, the rollout was just cause for celebration. That it ocurred significantly ahead of schedule, and with work on several more production machines progressing smoothly, was no doubt a relief; for less than a month earlier, the US Army had announced its desire to acquire a further 112 Apaches as part of the Fiscal Year 1984 (FY 84) US defence budget. When added to the 60 machines already contracted for (11 and 48 in Lots One and Two respectively), Hughes Helicopters now had orders for 171 production Apaches, the final example of which they were due to deliver in July 1986. An initial production rate of three

Above: With production in full swing, and with early teething troubles ironed out, Apaches began to roll off the assembly line in ever-greater numbers.

units per month was soon to be established; but with US Army plans at that time calling for the acquisition of some 515 AH-64As, the company was already looking to ways of achieving a peak production rate four times as great during the late-1980s.

The rollout ceremony must also have been tinged with sadness for many of the employees, for it was common knowledge that Hughes Helicopters had been put up for sale by its owners, the Summa Corporation. By the time that PV-01 made its maiden flight on 9 January 1984, the company had been sold to the McDonnell Douglas Corporation for $470 million. On 27 August 1984, Hughes Helicopters was renamed the McDonnell Douglas Helicopters (MDDH) Company.

TEAMWORK

Mention has already been made of Teledyne Ryan Aeronautical in connection with the manufacture of the Apache fuselage. In fact, although the completed Apache bears the stamp of MDDH, it is the sum of many parts assembled and supplied by a host of sub-contractors spread across the

---

A WINNER TAKES SHAPE

Paintshop: The cockpit structures are painted in a black conducive to night-time operations.
Station 1: The first electrical wiring is installed, as are both of the engine nacelles.
Station 2: The Nitrogen Inert System, armour-plating and more wiring are installed.
Station 3: More wiring and plating added.
Staion 4: Work on crew stations, including initial positioning of control linkages.
Staion 5: Linkless ammunition feed system installed; further work on flight controls.
Station 6: Pneumatic system, cockpit pedals and further wire harnesses installed.
Station 7: All landing gear units, one primary fuel cell and the vertical stabilizer installed.
Stations 8 & 9: Additional wiring plus work on control linkages.
Station 10: T700-GE-701 engines fitted.

Station 11: Main transmission and auxiliary power unit are installed.
Station 12: Addition of engine subsystems, including forward-mounted gear boxes.
Station 13: Testing of electrical systems.
Station 14: Crew cyclic sticks, a second fuel cell and circuit breaker panel added.
Station 15: Stub wings fitted; avionics and electrical ''black boxes'' are validated.
Station 16: Avionics suites and a set of engine fire extinguishers are added.
Station 17: Both crew seats and the area weapons systems are fitted; flight control rigging is undertaken. Various Production Test Procedures are also completed.
Station 18: Further systems testing.
Station 19: Evaluation of the Hellfire Modular Missile System and TADS/PNVS.

Station 20: Canopy transparency panels, body fairing and covers now in place.
Stations 21 & 22: The airframe is now painted and then left to dry.
Station 23: Main rotor blades and tail rotor driveshaft installed. Functional tests on the APU, fuel system etc.
Station 24: Production Acceptance Test Procedures carried out. If successful, the Apache will make its first flight.
Station 25: The US Army inspects and approves all log books, then conducts its own test programme.
Station 26: Configuration end-of-item inspections by MDDH and the US Army.
Station 27: The completed and tested Apache is signed over to the US Army, then flown off to its new home.

Above: On the line, technicians make use of a digital test meter (the small, pale-coloured box ahead of the canopy) to test the TADS/PNVS electrical wiring.

United States and abroad, known collectively as the Apache Industry Team. Together, they produce a truly awesome combat helicopter, the design and construction of which is based on three fundamental and crucial requirements of any successful weapons system deployed on or over the modern-day battlefield:
*Ballistic Tolerance
*Reduced Detectability
*Enhanced Manoeuvrability
As the largest element in the Apache's structure, the fuselage embodies much of the first of these elements. Divided into forward, centre and aft sections, it is a conventional semi-monocoque, aluminium-alloy structure, liberally embued with fracture-tough composite materials and

oversized structural members, as well as featuring redundant load paths. Together, these features form a fuselage designed to survive multiple hits from enemy fire, ranging from light machine-gun rounds to .90in (23mm) cannon shells.

SELF-PROTECTION

Specific components have also been designed with battlefield survivability in mind, most notably items forming part of the Apache's transmission system. In addition to armour protection in the form of electro-slag remelt (ESR) steel protective collars fitted to specific components, the Apache's main transmission is designed to continue functioning in the event of a catastrophic oil loss.

While the main gearboxes (located immediately ahead of each engine nacelle, and lubricated by dual-redundant systems to protect against single-feed failure) can continue to run

for up to an hour following an oil loss, the intermediate and tail rotor gearboxes are rendered virtually impervious to the effects of small-arms fire thanks to the use of grease rather than oil for onboard lubrication.

Not surprisingly, the two General Electric T700-GE-701 turbo-shaft engines also incorporate various survivability features. The most obvious concerns their location: widely separated in individual nacelles in an attempt to minimize the chances of single-strike damage affecting both powerplants, while at the same time offering the safety of full twin-engined redundancy. Again, key components feature armour-protection.

In addition to armour protection, the engines also have the advantage of

Below: Racing towards the camera, this Apache clearly reveals its widely-spaced engine nacelles; a configuration adopted to enhance battlefield survivability.

A Winner Takes Shape

McDonnell Douglas AH-64A Apache cutaway drawing key

1 Night systems sensor scanner
2 Pilot's Night Vision Sensor (PNVS) infra-red scanner
3 Electro-optical target designation and night sensor systems turret
4 Target acquisition and designation sight daylight scanner (TADS)
5 Azimuth motor housing
6 TADS/PNVS swivelling turret
7 Turret drive motor housing
8 Sensor turret mounting

9 Rear view mirror
10 Nose compartment access hatches
11 Remote terminal unit
12 Signal data converter
13 Co-pilot/gunner's yaw control rudder pedals
14 Forward radar warning antenna
15 Hughes M230A-1 Chain Gun barrel
16 Fuselage sponson fairing
17 Avionics cooling air ducting
18 Boron armoured cockpit flooring
19 Co-pilot/gunner's "fold-down" control column
20 Weapons control panel
21 Instrument panel shroud
22 Windscreen wiper

23 Co-pilot/gunner's armoured windscreen
24 Head-down sighting system viewfinder
25 Pilot's armoured windscreen panel
26 Windscreen wiper
27 Co-pilot/gunner's Kevlar armoured seat
28 Safety harness
29 Side console panel
30 Engine power levers
31 Avionics equipment bays, port and starboard
32 Avionics bay access door
33 Collective pitch control lever
34 Adjustable crash-resistant seat mountings
35 Pilot's rudder pedals
36 Cockpit side window panel

37 Pilot's instrument console
38 Inter-cockpit acrylic blast shield
39 Starboard side window entry hatches
40 Rocket launcher pack
41 Starboard wing stores pylons
42 Cockpit roof glazing
43 Instrument panel shroud
44 Pilot's Kevlar armoured seat
45 Collective pitch control lever
46 Side console panel
47 Engine power levers
48 Rear cockpit floor level
49 Main undercarriage shock absorber mounting
50 Linkless ammunition feed chute
51 Forward fuel tank; total fuel capacity 375 US gal (1,419 litre)
52 Control rod linkages
53 Cockpit ventilating air louvres
54 Display adjustment panel
55 Grab handles/maintenance steps
56 Control system hydraulic actuators (three)
57 Ventilating air intake
58 UHF aerial
59 Starboard stub wing
60 Main rotor blades
61 Laminated blade-root attachment joints
62 Vibration absorbers
63 Blade pitch bearing housing
64 Air data sensor mast
65 Rotor hub unit
66 Offset flapping hinges
67 Elastomeric lead/lag dampers

68 Blade pitch control rod
69 Pitch control swashplate
70 Main rotor mast
71 Air turbine starter/auxiliary power unit (APU) input shaft
72 Rotor head control mixing linkages
73 Gearbox mounting plate
74 Transmission oil coolers, port and starboard
75 Rotor brake
76 Main gearbox
77 Gearbox mounting struts
78 Generator
79 Input shaft from port engine
80 Gearbox mounting deck
81 Tail rotor control rod linkage
82 Ammunition magazine, 1,200 rounds
83 Stub wing attachment points
84 Engine transmission gearbox
85 Air intake
86 Engine integral oil tank
87 General Electric T700-GE-701 turboshaft engine
88 Intake particle separator
89 Engine accessory equipment gearbox
90 Oil cooler plenum
91 Gas turbine starter/APU
92 Starboard engine cowling panels/fold-down maintenance platform
93 Starboard engine exhaust ducts
94 APU exhaust
95 Pneumatic system and environmental control equipment

96 Cooling air exhaust louvres
97 Particle separator exhaust duct/mixer
98 "Black Hole" infra-red suppression engine exhaust ducts
99 Hydraulic reservoir
100 Gearbox/engine bay tail fairings
101 Internal maintenance platform
102 Tail rotor control rod
103 Spine shaft housing
104 Tail rotor transmission shaft
105 Shaft bearing and couplings
106 Bevel drive intermediate gearbox
107 Fin/rotor pylon construction
108 Tail rotor drive shafts
109 All-moving tailplane
110 Tail rotor gearbox housing
111 Right-angle final drive gearbox
112 Fin tip aerial fairing
113 Rear radar warning antennae
114 Tail navigation light
115 Cambered trailing-edge section (directional stability)
116 Tail rotor pitch actuator
117 Tail rotor hub mechanism
118 Assymetric (noise attenuation) tail rotor blades
119 Tailplane construction

120 Tailplane pivot bearing
121 Castoring tailwheel
122 Tailwheel shock absorber
123 Tailwheel yoke attachment
124 Handgrips/maintenance steps
125 Tailplane control hydraulic jack

126 Fin/rotor pylon attachment joint
127 Chaff/flare dispenser
128 Tailboom ring frames
129 Ventral radar warning aerial
130 Tailcone frame and stringer construction
131 UHF aerial
132 Automatic Direction Finding (ADF) loop aerial
133 ADF sense aerial
134 Access hatch
135 Handgrips/maintenance steps
136 Radio and electronics equipment bay
137 Rear fuel tank
138 Reticulated foam fire suppressant tank bay linings
139 VHF aerial
140 Main rotor blade stainless steel spars (five)
141 Glass-fibre spar linings

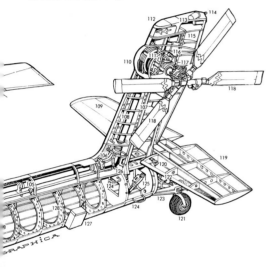

142 Honeycomb trailing-edge panel
143 Glass-fibre blade skins
144 Trailing-edge fixed tab
145 Swept blade tip fairing
146 Static discharger
147 Stub wing trailing-edge flap
148 Stub wing rib construction
149 Twin spar booms
150 Port navigation and strobe lights
151 Port wing stores pylons
152 Rocket pack: nineteen 2.75in (7cm) FFAR rockets
153 Rockwell AGM-114A Hellfire anti-tank missiles
154 Missile launch rails
155 Fuselage sponson aft fairing
156 Boarding step
157 Port mainwheel
158 Main undercarriage leg strut
159 Shock absorber strut
160 Boarding steps
161 Main undercarriage leg pivot fixing
162 Ammunition feed and cartridge case return chutes
163 Gun swivelling mounting
164 Azimuth control mounting frame
165 Hughes M230A-1 Chain Gun 30mm automatic cannon
166 Blast suppression cannon muzzle

being housed within protective nacelles. However, the four-bladed, fully-articulated main rotor system remains exposed. Nevertheless, it is a strong unit. The steel and aluminium main rotor hub supports each of the four blades via a laminated strap retention system consisting of 22 laminates, up to 10 of which can fail with no effect on the load-carrying abilities of the strap assembly itself.

Above: In contrast to much of the state-of-the-art technology aboard the Apache, the fully-articulated main rotor is a most conservative configuration.

In addition, each of the rotor blades is a very tough, ballistically tolerant structure in itself. Comprising five overlapping stainless steel spars lined with structural glass-fibre tubes, the

Above: The importance of built-in battlefield survivability for the Apache's main rotor blades cannot be overstressed, and this photo clearly demonstrates the blades' ability to survive the impact of a hit on the titanium leading-edge and the glass-fibre interior.

A Winner Takes Shape

forward half and leading-edge of each blade is covered with a laminated stainless steel skin, while the rear half is made up of composite materials. The result is a structure with a fatigue life in excess of 4,500 flying hours.

But should enemy fire result in a loss of oil pressure in one or both engines, lubrication can be maintained via a self-contained dry sump system for each powerplant. Small reservoirs of oil built into each sump can be bled out, atomized with air jets, then fed to engine bearings in the form of a fine oil mist for up to 30 seconds duration.

Of course, any such built-in structural/component "hardening" can

SPECIFICATION

McDonnell Douglas AH-64A Apache

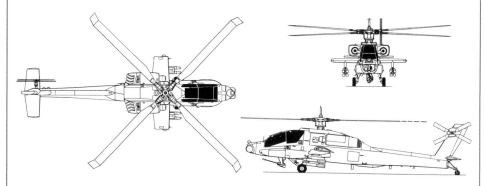

Dimensions
Length overall: 58ft 3in (17.77m)
Height: 15ft 3½in (4.67m)
Wing span: 17ft 2in (5.24m)
Tailplane span: 11ft 2in (3.41m)
Main rotor diameter: 48ft 0in (14.64m)

Weights
Empty: 10,760lb (4,885kg)
Mission gross: 14,445lb (6,558kg)
Maximum external stores: 1,700lb (772kg)
Maximum take-off: 21,000lb (9,534kg)

Power
2×General Electric T700-GE-701 turboshaft engines
Power rating per engine 1,696shp (1,265kW)

Power rating, one engine out: 1,723shp (1,285kW)
Internal fuel: 376 US gal (1,423 litre)
External fuel: 816 US gal (3,089 litre)

Performance
Maximum level speed: 184mph (296km/h)
Never-exceed speed 227mph (365km/h)
Service ceiling: 21,000ft (6,405m)
Service ceiling, one engine out: 10,800ft (3,294m)
Rate of climb, at sea level: 2,500ft/min (762.5m/min)
Maximum range, internal fuel only: 300 miles (483km)
Ferry range, internal & external fuel: 1,057 miles (1,701km)

Above: Secure in their seats, the Apache crewmen are protected by Kevlar side-shields, boron plates and a transparent blast shield.

only really prove its worth if at least one of the two crewmen up front is capable of flying the helicopter. Should the crew sucumb to enemy fire, any such built-in ballistic tolerance will all too quickly be rendered redundant in the most literal sense of the word. But here too, the designers of the Apache have given much thought as to how to enhance the Apache's built-in crash-worthiness, with the aim of achieving two basic goals — save the crew, and repair the Apache to fight again.

These goals are reflected in the construction of the tandem cockpits, wherein protection of the individual crewmen is of paramount concern. Lightweight but immensely tough Kevlar forms the protective "armour" for both seats, and is supplemented by lightweight boron shields built into the floor and sides of each cockpit as protection against high-explosive and/or armour-piercing projectiles.

Boron armour shields are also positioned between the individual cockpits, as is a transparent acrylic blast shield.

Apache crew protection

Right: The Apache was designed to set new standards of protection and survivability in the modern battlefield.

■ Crew compartment armour
■ Blast/Fragment shield
□ Transparent blast shield

This latter item serves a dual purpose. On the one hand, it separates the two cockpits and their respective crew, thus reducing the risk of a single hit in the cockpit area incapacitating both crew. Additionally, the blast barrier forms part of an integral roll-bar in conjunction with the canopy cover in the event of a crash-landing. Should the Apache be forced down in such circumstances, this rollbar is just one element designed to give the crew a 95 per cent chance of surviving a hard crash-landing. Already heavily protected, both crew seats are designed to survive a vertical impact of up to 42ft/sec (12.80m/sec) by absorbing up to two-thirds of the 37g force applied to the cockpit floor at this rate of descent, thus "cushioning" both crewmen.

Their chances of survival are further enhanced by a built-in design feature of the M230E-1 Chain Gun. Located under the forward fuselage, the gun's mounting is designed to collapse up and into the fuselage area between the two cockpits on impact, thus avoiding striking either of the crew.

The Apache's three-point landing gear is also designed to help absorb some of the force of a high-impact crash-landing, with the two main trailing-arm units capable of absorbing rates of vertical impact of up to 42ft/sec (12.80m/sec).

Internally, the two fuel cells located in the lower area of the forward and centre fuselage sections, and with a combined capacity of 376 US gal (1,423 litres), are crash-resistant and self-sealing, thus significantly reducing the risk of a post-impact, onboard fire.

HIDDEN HUNTER

The second basic operational requirement incorporated in the design and manufacture of the Apache is the need to minimize its overall detectability in the face of a host of hi-tech surveillance and armament systems deployed by the enemy on the modern battlefield. With this in mind, several built-in features help to significantly reduce the Apache's visual, aural, radar and Infra-Red (IR) signatures.

Visually, too many previous helicopters operating over the battlefield have given their position away unintentionally due to tell-tale glints as light bounces off their smooth, rounded canopy glazing. The lesson has been learnt the hard way, not least by the US Army, with the result that the Apache (as well as several current models of the AH-1 Cobra) sports flat-plate cockpit glazing which significantly reduces the incidence and likelihood of "glint giveaway".

In addition, a check of the Apache's airframe dimensions reveals a quite slender beast which, when combined with highly effective nap-of-the-earth (NOE) flying and concealment tactics, is extremely difficult for an enemy to acquire visually — until it's too late.

However, the effectiveness of such visual concealment can easily be negated if the helicopter's rotor system produces that all too familiar "thwack" as the main and tail rotor blades cut through the air. The UH-1 and AH-1 are classic examples of such "hear them before you see them" helicopters, although some attempt has been made to reduce their very noisy rotor "slap".

Above: Unique to the Apache, the twin, double-bladed tail rotor assemblies maximize the use of pre-determined deflection angles in an attempt to minimize the tell-tale rotor "slap".

A Winner Takes Shape

Right: The outward canting of the "Black Hole" engine exhaust ducts helps direct the hot engine gases away from the airframe to reduce the Apache's IR signature.

As already noted in this Chapter, particular attention was paid in the design of the Apache to the benefits of redundancy within the airframe itself, and this philosophy is further illustrated in the operative systems. When it comes to the back-up flight control system — arguably the most important onboard system of all — a bold decision was taken to adopt a fly-by-wire (FBW) back-up control system (BUCS) in preference to a more conventional, dual-redundant mechanical system. The former is far lighter and bestows a far greater degree of inflight safety, and can be checked electronically before each flight to confirm its operational integrity.

The BUCS operates through the electromechanical valves located on the flight-control actuators, and also makes use of the digital automatic stabilization equipment (DASE) package which, like the BUCS, is produced by the Sperry Corporation. The latter

package improves all aspects of the Apache's flying and handling qualities by adding damping, refining the coordinates of turns, tailoring all inputs and providing an attitude-hold and a hover position relative to the ground whenever the pilot requests it.

Should the primary Parker-Bertea mechanical FCS be severed or jamm-

ed by hostile fire, the BUCS is automatically engaged. As a direct result of such an action, the DASE takes an electrical signal from a special linear variable differential transformer (LVDT) located in the cockpit, processes it and relays it to the control actuator. The latter responds to the LVDT input, enabling the pilot to maintain control of the Apache.

PERFORMANCE

There can be no doubting the comprehensive nature of these built-in features and systems, and they are complemented by the Apache's quite awesome flight performance capabilities. The best measure of a helicopter's performance (at pressurized mission weight, atmosphere and endurance) are its vertical rate-of-climb (VRoC), airspeed and agility, all of which are combined in a flight envelope.

From the outset, the Apache had to achieve a stiff set of flight performance goals, with a VRoC (while carrying eight Hellfire missiles and the Chain Gun) of 450ft/min (137m/min) at 4,000ft (1,220m) above sea level and 95deg F. A cruising speed of 168mph (279km/h) at the same altitude was further stipulated, as was a mission endurance of 1h 50min.

In reality, the Apache can rapidly accelerate and manoeuver to avoid being engaged by hostile air defence forces, pulling up to 3.5g at low altitude (most combat helicopters cannot exceed 2g). In laymans terms, the Apache possesses the ability to execute extremely quick, tight turns, and accelerate away from danger. At least

Left: Though primarily used for the carriage of weapons, the four underwing pylons can also carry 230 US gal (871l) tanks, thus greatly increasing the Apache's abilities to deploy on its own.

one prototype has exceeded a speed of 240mph (386km/h) in a dive.

Worldwide operations are further enhanced by the ability to operate in ambient temperatures ranging from -25deg F to +125deg F without special modifications, although the extremely harsh conditions encountered during the Apache's recent deployment in Kuwait and Saudi Arabia, in particular the debilitating effects of the sand on the leading edges of the main and tail rotor blades, have tested some of these "facts and figures" to the full.

The results, it has to be said, have not all been positive, and the Apache performance continues to arouse strong passions, particularly on Capitol Hill. A recent US Congress General Accounting Office (GAO) report on the Apache's reliability in the field was severely critical, even going so far as to suggest that the US Army's anti-tank operations and tactics were all but useless due to a severe lack of Apaches that were serviced and ready for battle.

SERVICE PROBLEMS

The report concluded that, on the basis of a survey of 11 US Army Apache-equipped units based in the USA and Germany conducted between January 1989 and April 1990, the average availability rate was just 50% — and that this figure would fall still further should actual combat be entered into.

Compared to the USMC's AH-1 fleet figure of 27.7hrs, the US Army's Apache force was averaging just under 13hrs flight-time per month. In addition, 8-13 maintenance man hours

Right: Superb manoeuvreability is an important asset to the Apache. Its maximum rate of roll touches 100deg/sec — a figure more akin to that of a modern-day fighter than a helicopter.

were required for every flight hour, compared to a figure of 5.5 per flight hour established during OT-II testing in 1981.

The GAO report concluded that the US Army should forego any plans to purchase further Apaches, and should invest instead in more support person-

Left: By opening the throttles and pushing the nose down, the massive power reserves of the two T700 engines combine to produce excellent acceleration.

nel, spare parts and test equipment. The Army, however, has countered many of the so-called facts in the GAO report, pointing to the sheer sophistication of the Apache as a partial explaination. In addition, a combined MDDH/Army troubleshooting programme led to an announcement in April 1990 that six out of the ten most serious faults had been fixed, and that remedies for the other four had been identified.

In reality, the Apache has long been a political "hot potato" and will likely remain so for the rest of its operational life, although initial reports of staggering successes during Operation "Desert Storm" may help defray such attacks. For the US Army, confidence is high, and the service has already signalled its future intentions with plans to acquire a major new Apache variant for operational deployment in the 1990s. The AH-64 is set to stay in service for many years.

"THE Apache will change the way the Army fights. Its contribution to battle will be as significant as the introduction of the tank."

High praise indeed from Lt. Gen. Crosbie E. Saint, Commander III Corps and Fort Hood, Texas, yet an accurate assessment of the AH-64A's awesome fighting abilities. But with an ever-increasing variety of attack helicopters on offer, what is it that makes the Apache the undisputed champion of the world? Certainly the extremely strong and survivable airframe, analyzed in the previous chapter, provides part of the answer; but the crucial features that set this airborne warrior apart concern its potent range of weapons (the subject of this chapter) and the array of hi-tech sensors — the visionics — used to maximize the Apache's lethality in battle.

At the outset of its AAH programme, the US Army made it clear that it was looking for a helicopter whose primary mission was to "kill" enemy armour, specifically Main Battle Tanks (MBTs). In the early stages of the AAH programme, the weapon system chosen to fulfill this primary mission requirement was an air-launched version of the tried and tested Hughes BGM-71 TOW anti-armour missile; and the winner of the helicopter fly-off was to have been configured to utilize this system.

However, TOW is merely an acronym for Tube-launched, Optically-tracked, Wire-guided; and therein lies the missile's fundamental weakness. Once launched, the gunner has to control the missile, guiding it all the way to the target via a series of steering commands transmitted to the missile via long control wires attached to the missile at one end and to its launch tube at the other. For the missile to be guided to the target successfully, the gunner has to establish a clear and direct line-of-sight (LOS) with the target itself — and that leaves the helicopter open and exposed to the ravages of enemy anti-aircraft fire. Needless to say, the Army dearly wanted to find a system that would lessen such exposure.

Work on such "fire-and-forget" air-launched, anti-tank missile systems had been carried out during the 1960s by several companies, including Rockwell with its ZAGM-64A Hornet. But though it had potential, the Hornet was cancelled in 1968. Nevertheless, the Army's requirement for such a missile was very much alive, and by 1970, Rockwell had revived the Hornet to act as a test-bed for various seeker systems as part of a new programme known as Hellfire: HELicopter-Launched, FIRE-and-forget.

The seekers under test during the early-1970s included laser, TV-guided and Infra-red (IR) units, and the programme soon established that here was a system with much potential for future development. The eventual result was a bold decision taken by the US Army on 26 February 1976 to abandon the TOW missile in favour of the Rockwell model. Accordingly, the company was awarded a full-scale engineering development contract in October 1976 for a laser-guided model of what was to be known as the

Left: Built around three primary weapons, namely the Hellfire air-to-ground missile, aerial rocket and 30mm cannon, the Apache is a lethal warrior second to none.

Rockwell AGM-114A Hellfire

Right: Weighing in at less than 100lb (45.4kg), just under one-sixth of the Hellfire's weight is taken up by the shaped charged warhead located behind the nose-mounted, semi-active laser seeker. Upon detonation, a jet of hot gas is forced forward and into the penetrated target's interior.

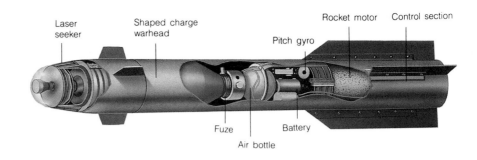

Rockwell AGM-114A Hellfire Modular Missile System (HMMS). Two months later, the YAH-64A was announced as winner of the US Army's AAH fly-off competition.

Initial test firings were conducted by HueyCobras, but by May 1979, five missiles had been launched by AV-02 at MCAS Camp Pendleton. These firings comprised two from the ground, one in the hover, and two during forward flight. Later, the Yuma Proving Ground was the setting for more launches, this time in conjunction with ground-based laser designators (GBLDs) to illuminate targets. By the time the first production AH-64A Apache was ready for delivery, no less than 72 AGM-114A Hellfires had been launched in a comprehensive test programme. Hellfire was a winner.

Measuring 5ft 4in (1.62m) in length and weighing in at 98.5lb (44.7kg), Hellfire is a solid-propellant, terminally-guided weapon. Just under one sixth of its weight is taken up by a 17lb (7.7kg) conical-shaped, hollow-charge warhead, which can penetrate enemy armour to a depth of 27.5in (70cm). To achieve this impressive feat, Hellfire travels at supersonic speeds up to 888mph (1,429km/h), powered by either a mini-smoke or extended-range pulsed rocket motor.

SEEK AND DESTROY

Unclassified figures indicate a range in excess of five miles (8km), with the ability to be launched at sea level or at the Apache's service ceiling of 21,000ft (6,405m), and while the heli-copter is hovering or travelling at maximum speed. Highly manoeuvrable, Hellfire can pull turns of up to 13g while in supersonic flight; and once it hits the target, the armour-piercing (AP) warhead is forced straight through the guidance system and into the enemy armour.

Hellfire's impressive range allows the Apache to launch its missiles from stand-off positions, thus retaining the element of surprise when confronting potentially large numbers of highly mobile MBTs and their attendant anti-aircraft units. Just how the missile's guidance system is used in conjunction with the Apache's onboard sensors during an attack will be covered in the next chapter, but it is worth noting now that Hellfire's modular design has allowed several other forms of seeker

Above: Nobody can doubt the great advances made in recent years in the area of tank armour-plating. Unfortunately, no-one told the Hellfire . . .

. . . and as the Iraqi Army has recently found out, Soviet-built MBTs are disturbingly vulnerable to the Apache's primary "arrow", seen here about to hit . . .

. . . followed just a fraction of a second after penetration of the armour-plating by the inevitable explosion, as the tank "brews up". There is simply no escape.

Tools For The Trade

Right: With most sorties against Iraqi armour during *"Desert Storm"* conducted from rough-field sites, the Hellfire's light weight eased in-field reloading.

head to be tried and tested as alternatives to the laser guidance system.

Specifically, these have included Infra-Red (IR), Radio Frequency/Infra-Red (RF/IR), Imaging Infra-Red (IIR), Millimetre wavelength (MM-W) and dual mode IIR/MM-W seeker head systems.

Consequently, a new Hellfire model with enhanced "fire-and-forget" capabilities based on the use of an RF seeker head is now in development by Martin Marietta Missile Systems. Known officially as the Hellfire Optimized Missile System (HOMS), the new model features a stronger warhead to beat the best armour-plating deployed by the enemy, plus a seeker head "hardened" against advanced electro-optical countermeasures. As a spokesman for the US Army's Missile Command put it succinctly: "Basically, we're looking for ways to improve the lethality of the weapon."

Just as important, HOMS will be compatible with the MM-W radar be-

ing developed by Martin-Marietta and Westinghouse for use by an advanced version of the AH-64A known as the Longbow Apache (see next chapter).

Martin Marietta, winner over Rockwell International in an Army competition to choose the best configuration for HOMS, is now involved in a 27-month research and development programme that includes 65 HOMS test firings. These are expected to start in late-1991 and, if successful, could be followed by full-scale production of this enhanced-capability missile system starting as early as 1993. At stake are production options currently covering at least 11,000 missiles, these to form the Apache/Longbow Apache's primary anti-tank armament well into the 21st Century.

FIRE SUPPRESSION

While Hellfire endows the Apache with a point suppression capability, the helicopter's secondary armament sub-system is designed primarily for area defence suppression, although it also possesses the ability to neutralize lightly-armoured and soft-skinned targets if necessary.

This ability, similar in concept to the fire suppression practised by the first and second generation of helicopter "gunships", comes courtesy of two weapons: the M230E-1 1.2in

(30mm) Chain Gun and the 2.75in (70mm) unguided folding-fin aerial rocket (FFAR).

The Hughes M230E-1 Chain Gun is a single-barrel, automatic cannon measuring 5ft 5in (1.65m) and weighing a hefty 118lb (53.6kg). Its evolution closely shadowed that of the Apache itself, and it too was involved in a head-to-head competition with a rival, namely the General Electric XM188 three-barrel cannon. Known then as the XM230, the Hughes design was named the Chain Gun by virtue of its rotating-bolt mechanism, which is electrically driven during firing by an extremely simple — almost

Above: A compact, single-barrel weapon, the M230E-1 Chain Gun and its support mechanism were designed with practicality in overhaul and reloading in mind.

Above: Fed from an ammunition bay located beneath the main rotor mast, the Chain Gun can loose off its 30mm shells at up to 650 rounds per-minute.

rudimentary — chain drive. With all the moving parts keyed together, the result is fully controlled and precisely timed movement when activated.

Like its predecessors, the Chain Gun is mounted in an undernose position, but much further aft than the weapons carried by, say, the AH-1 HueyCobra family. The Chain Gun is also different in that it is not encased in a protective turret. Instead, it lies in what can best be described as a supporting cradle. In the event of a high-impact crash-landing, the entire unit is designed to "collapse" upwards and into the fuselage space between the CP/G and pilot.

The M230s "punch" is provided by 1.2in (30mm) XM799 high-explosive (HE) or XM789 high-explosive dual-purpose (HEDP) linkless ammunition, this being stored in the fuselage area behind the cockpits and beneath the Apache's main transmission. This positioning is important, for with up to 1,200 rounds of ammunition weighing in at some 2,100lb (953kg), maintaining the Apache's centre of gravity is vital if the marked changes in trim generated during gun-firing are to be compensated for. Such considerations also account in part for the set-back location of the Chain Gun.

Normal rate of fire for the M230 is 625rpm, although this can be increased to 650rpm. Just what quantity of ammunition will be carried depends on the overall weapons configuration for each mission profile (1,200 rounds is the maximum, but some missions envisage only 320 rounds being carried). Fire rates will vary according to requirements, but one cycle programme is based on a series of six 50-round bursts, each with a five-

second interval, followed by a ten-minute muzzle-cooling period.

Muzzle velocity is a highly impressive 2,650ft/sec (808m/sec), and the stated range is in the order of 13,100ft (4,000m). The gun is hydraulically driven and remote-controlled, and can be slewed through 110deg either side of the centreline, as well as +11/-60deg in elevation. As with Hellfire, so the Chain Gun can be slaved to the Apache's onboard sensors. These in turn can be slaved to the Integrated Helmet And Display Sighting System (IHADSS) worn by both pilot and CP/G. Alternatively, the latter crew member can aim and fire the Chain Gun manually.

The third element in the Apache's offensive armament package, and the second element to be used as an area suppression weapon, is also the most basic system, namely the long-serving 2.75in (70mm) FFAR, which forms part of the Aerial Rocket Control System (ARCS).

Up to 76 of these simple but effective rockets can be carried in four

Right: Though officially unguided, the folding-fin aerial rockets spin up in their tubes prior to launch, thus maximizing target-strike accuracy once fired.

Tools For The Trade

These then are the Apache's three principle weapon systems, which account for the lion's share of the fearsome reputation earned by this attack helicopter in the heat of battle, not least during the recent blitz of Iraqi hard- and soft-skinned targets during Operation "*Desert Storm*".

But they are by no means the only "arrows" in the Apache's quiver, for strenuous efforts have been made in recent years to enhance its combat capabilities by means of other weapons, most notably AAMs to bestow an air defence capability. The addition of AAMs such as the Sidewinder and Stinger signal the growing importance being placed on the formulation of effective air-to-air, anti-helicopter combat tactics, and the need for the Apache to be able to conduct such operations against potential adversaries such as the Mil Mi-24 Hind, Mi-28 Havoc and Kamov Ka-41 Hokum.

The tried and trusted Raytheon AIM-9 Sidewinder was first fired from an Apache as long ago as 1988, and there can be little doubt as to its merits. In its AIM-9L form, complete with all-aspect acquisition and in-terception capabilities, as well as a more powerful motor and a 23lb (10.4kg) warhead, it represented a significant addition to the Apache's varied armoury.

The US Army, however, always perceived the Sidewinder as an interim AAM, in lieu of the combat qualification of a more suitable weapon. Fundamental limitations in the use of this 1950s-vintage missile, most notably its unsuitability for launch in NOE conditions because of the need to drop the missile clear of its pylon before ignition of the rocket motor, thus necessitating exposure of the Apache for optimum launch conditions, clearly limited its operational effectiveness in the anti-helicopter role.

The remedy to this operational shortfall comes in the form of a far more suitable weapon, namely an air-launched derivative of the US Army's man-portable, shoulder-mounted FIM-92 Stinger missile system, Like the Sidewinder, the tube-launched Air-To-Air Stinger (ATAS) is mounted on the Apache's wing-tips, but is a far more compact weapon. A normal load consists of four such missiles (two per wing-tip, stacked vertically).

Integration of the ATAS with the Apache began in September 1987, with the first test-firing conducted one year later, and it was soon clear that, if successful, it could offer a major step forward in attempts to secure an effective and credible air-to-air defence capability for the Apache.

The compactness of the ATAS is further reflected in the size of its warhead — just 2lb (0.9kg) compared to the Sidewinder's 23lb (10.4kg) unit — although the US Army is confident in the missile's ability to knock out its primary heliborne targets. In addition, the ATAS embodies its own IR target seeker and all-aspect homing capabilities. The result, when combined with the Apache's excellent operational agility, is a highly potent self-defence capability.

Mention should also be made of the Bombardier Shorts Helstreak, a helicopter-launched derivative of the Starstreak close-combat, high-velocity,

Below: Though always seen as an interim addition in lieu of the arrival of Stinger, the AIM-9 Sidewinder proved the concept of the AAM-carrying Apache.

Right: Admittedly this Bell UH-1 was a captive target, but its sorry state merely confirms the inherent potency of Stinger.

ground-launched missile. Though real-life test firings have yet to be conducted, the manufacturer has teamed up with MDDH to promote this laser-guided, Mach 3-5-capable missile for use in conjunction with the Apache, most notably aboard any such machines acquired and operated by Great Britain's Army Air Corps.

Publicity material relating to Helstreak has also alluded to an additional — though modest — air-to-ground capability; but a more substantial alternative to the Apache's ''heavy metal'' — the Hellfire AGM — has recently been proposed in the shape of the AGM-65 Maverick missile.

Tested during 1990 (aboard an AH-1W), the Maverick has proved its

Below: An artist's impression of Stinger-equipped Apaches firing their missiles in anger. Note the distinctive stacked arrangement of the wing-tip launch tubes.

viability as a stand-off weapon for the US Army's Apache force, claims the Hughes Missile Systems Group. Up to four such missiles could be carried, one per underwing pylon, and be fitted with either a 300lb (136kg) penetrator warhead or a 125lb (57kg) shaped charge warhead, as well as individual IR seeker heads slaved to the Apache's TADS. An autonomous

MM-W seeker head is also under development to enable compatibility with the Longow Apache's versatile fire-control system.

However, at the time of writing, the US Army has not announced any official requirement for the Maverick AGM, and with an ever-decreasing Defence Budget, its adoption has to be seen as unlikely at best.

FOR all its undoubted capabilities in the heat of battle, even the most vociferous proponents of the Apache could hardly disagree with the opinion that it is a thoroughly ugly helicopter. Many an author has alluded to its similarity in appearance to an insect, and when viewed from a head-on perspective, one can easily see why such a description comes to mind: the wings are there, as are the legs, and the uncompromising lines surrounding the stepped cockpits can, with just a little imagination, begin to take on the appearance of a particularly malevolent "face". But it is what lies ahead of these features that draws the most comment; no smooth nose contours, rather some closely-grouped "lumps and bumps" that form a set of super-powerful, all-seeing eyes.

Among the hard lessons learnt by the US Army during the Vietnam War was the fact that any future anti-armour helicopter should be able to launch attacks by day and night, and be able to conduct such operations in marginal weather conditions. As the AAH programme evolved, and the Apache took shape, so these operational requirements manifested themselves in a package of state-of-the-art, nose-mounted electro-optical sensors, popularly referred to as the Apache's "visionics".

The logic behind the development and inclusion of these target acquisition subsystems was both simple and practical: if the Apache was to succeed in delivering an effective "punch" to counter the ranks of highly-mobile WarPac armour poised to sweep westward across the plains of Northern Europe, every round of ordnance, be it rocket, missile or bullet, had to have an optimum chance of finding its assigned target.

That Northern Europe was seen as the Apache's most likely "killing field" was significant, for in addition to being able to operate around the clock — why would an enemy tank commander spurn the opportunity to make full use of the cloak of darkness to conceal the movement of his forces? — the notoriously unpredictable weather conditions had to be taken into account.

So it was that the US Army laid down a set of strict operational parameters for the visionics suite, including the ability to locate, identify and prosecute targets at a range of half a mile (0.80km), and with low cloud reducing the service ceiling to just 200ft (61m).

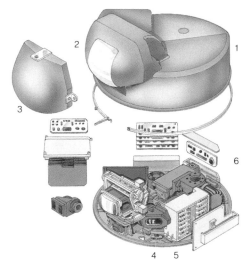

Above: Mounted in its own small turret atop the Apache's nose the AN/AAQ-11 Mk.III PNVS is built around five principal elements. These consist of a shroud (1); elevation mirror and lens assembly (2); window cover (3); IR imager (4); a focussing mechanism (5); and a focus control mechanism (6).

With the winner of the airframe competition announced, Phase II of the AAH programme drew a stage closer. Commencing in January 1977, this would see AV-02 and AV-03 used as flying test-beds for the rival Northrop and Martin Marietta Aerospace sensor subsystems, with the latter contractor declared the winner on 30 April 1980. Officially designated the Target Acquisition Designation Sight and Pilot Night Vision Sensor (TADS(PNVS), the sensors bestow the Apache with the ability to navigate to

Above: Often described as giving the Apache a bug-eye appearance, the TADS/PNVS turret can best be described as odd-looking but awesomely effective.

Above: Relatively spacious and uncluttered, the rear cockpit is occupied by the pilot. The screen with green symbology is the Video Display Unit.

the target area quickly and discreetly (by means of NOE flying), and to then launch attacks from stand-off ranges against clearly identified targets by day or night, and in limited adverse weather conditions.

THE MAGIC BOX

Just what constitutes this nose-mounted box (or rather barrel), of tricks, and how the elements are used to enhance the Apache's versatility and fighting prowess, can best be described by analyzing the roles and capabilities of the individual elements that comprise the TADS/PNVS by an Apache during a sortie.

The first element to be used on a mission is the AN/AAQ-11 Mk.III PNVS. Located in its own turret atop the TADS horizontal barrel, it is the

Right: The TADS' day sensors share two optical ports. The DTV and laser operate through the upper, while the lower is the domain of the DVO.

smaller and simpler of the subsystems, and is used to get the crew and helicopter to the target area in the aforementioned marginal lighting and weather conditions.

FLY-BY-NIGHT

Built around a wide-angle (30deg x 40deg) field-of-view forward-looking infra-red (FLIR) sensor, the PNVS provides the pilot with a real-time thermal image of the panoramic scene before him, with the FLIR allowing him to fly and navigate by night. Of course, looking straight ahead, even with a wide-angle field-of-view, is of limited use in itself; thus a respectable degree of mobility has been built into the seeker head. In elevation it can travel between +25deg/-45deg, and in azimuth 90deg left or right of the centreline. All movements are conducted independent of the TADS barrel below, and can be executed with surprising speed thanks to a slew rate of up to 93deg/sec and 120deg/sec in elevation and azimuth respectively.

The thermal imagery acquired by the PNVS FLIR can be viewed by the · pilot in one of two ways. The first is via a cathode ray tube (CRT) known as the Video Display Unit (VDU), centrally located in his forward instru-

Above: The CP/Gs cockpit is dominated by the centrally-mounted sensor eyepiece, a display screen below and side-mounted hand controls.

ment console; the second is via yet another piece of technological wizardry, namely Honeywell Aerospace's Integated Helmet And Display Sighting System (IHADSS).

Easily distinguishable from more conventional "bone domes" by virtue of the electro-optical package that culminates in a distinctive stalk covering the right side of the wearer's face, IHADSS conveys a two-dimensional

TADS/PNVS optical paths

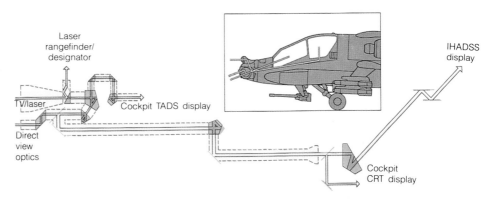

The Eyes Have It

Above: An IIR view of terrain ahead from the PNVS. Flight data is imposed on the image and the whole can be viewed using the pilot's helmet-mounted display.

video-form image of the area being scanned to the pilot via a small combiner glass positioned at the end of the stalk, just ahead of his right eye. Onto this image can be superimposed relevant symbology, e.g. airspeed and heading, thus enabling the pilot to fly and fight "heads up".

The inherent mobility of the PNVS turret in elevation and azimuth assumes a further significance in relation to the IHADSS unit, as the former's movement can be slaved to the latter, thus allowing the pilot to dictate the area to be scanned: if he wants to see what lies ahead at 45deg to port, all he has to do is turn his head to the said point — the PNVS turret will automatically turn to view

Above: The TADS turret contains direct view optics, TV and FLIR. The latter is seen here, and is used to engage targets at night, through smoke or in bad weather.

the same area and thus "see" the same scene.

In addition, the IHADSS system can be worn with equal effectiveness by the CP/G. The benefits are twofold: should the pilot be incapacitated during a mission, the thermal imagery provided by the PNVS will allow him to find his way home; while as a two-man team, one member can "show" a video image to the other, or can cue his partner's line of sight to a point or object of particular interest.

LOCK-ON

However this versatile unit is used to get to the battle area, once there and within range of potential targets, the second and largest element in the Apache's nose-mounted sensor package — TADS — comes into its own, enabling the CP/G in the Apache's front cockpit to acquire a target and receive all the fire control data necessary for the Apache's on-board weapon systems.

The unit consists of a barrel-like horizontal turret housing various sensor subsystems and the motor to facilitate movements in the azimuth. Like the PNVS above, it can be rotated in both elevation (+30deg/-60deg) and azimuth (120deg). Additionally, three electronic units are housed in the avionics bay and an optical relay tube (ORT) is located in the CP/Gs cockpit, with controls located on handgrips either side of the tube itself.

Having arrived at the battle area, TADS is used first and foremost to seek out, locate, and designate by laser (often referred to as "painting") potential targets. This is where the CP/G comes into his own, for the system allows him to acquire and track targets by day or night, and at stand-off distances outside the range of anti-aircraft defences such as the fearsome ZSU-23-4. To further enhance the

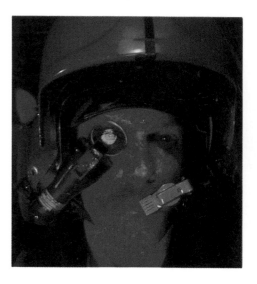

Above: Matching the technology of the Apache's sensors, the IHADSS unit can be used by both pilot and CP/G. Note the compact "display" screen.

scope of operational effectiveness, the CP/G can utilize TADS in conjunction with either a "heads up" (IHADSS) or "heads down" (ORT) display.

Looking at the Apache head-on, the TADS turret is clearly divided into port and starboard optics, this split reflecting the TADS' dual day and night sensor configuration. Each set of optics has its own distinctive glazing to protect the delicate sensors behind. The starboard half (looking head-on) is fronted by the smaller, blue-tint glazing that covers the daylight sensor package of four elements.

ELECTRONIC "EYES"

Mounted low in this optical port, the Direct View Optics (DVO) convey a visual image to the CP/G via an Optical Relay Tube (ORT), which terminates in a prominent eyepiece mounted on his forward instrument console. What the CP/G sees will depend on which of the two DVO field-of-view settings he selects: an 18deg

Above: The high quality of the images presented to the crew by TADS/PNVS enable them to fly NOE mission profiles with the greatest of confidence.

scan at a low-power setting of x3.5 magnification for a wide-angle scan search; or a much narrower 4deg scan at x16 magnification to allow him to study a potential target more closely and to assist in the precise guidance of ordnance.

In sharp contrast, a 4deg scan is the *maximum* field-of-view for the second element, namely the Daylight Television (DTV). A further two, even narrower settings can be selected, one at 0.9deg and the other a pencil beam scan setting of just 0.45deg. However, the principal benefit offered by the DTV is its ability to operate in the near-IR spectrum, thus allowing improved penetration of battlefield obscurants such as smoke, haze and mist, which would noticeably degrade the operational capabilities of the DVO subsystem.

Once a target has been acquired by the CP/G, whether via the DVO or DTV, it can subsequently be tracked automatically or manually. This allows the third element in the TADS'

daytime suite, the Laser Rangefinder/ Designator (LR/D), to enter the fray. This precision-boresighted element can be used to verify the target's range and to mark (or "paint") it with laser light. An active laser, the LR/D is aimed by the CP/G via the TADS turret, allowing him to place a laser spot precisely on the selected target (e.g. on the turret of a tank) for the benefit of laser-guided ordnance such as the Hellfire missile.

The ordnance, whether it be fired from the host Apache as part of an autonomous attack, or as part of a remote attack by another machine hiding behind natural cover, will seek out and lock onto the pulse code pro-

grammed into each beam. This operational capability can also be used to guide other laser-homing munitions, such as the Copperhead artillery shell, to their "painted" targets.

RIDING THE BEAM

The fourth daylight element is also the second to be based on laser light. Known as the Laser Spot Tracker (LST), it is a passive receiver used to locate targets "painted" by independent ground or airborne lasers. The LST scans for and finds friendly remote laser reflections, locking onto their emissions from the victim and passing all the relevant target data onto the CP/G via his cockpit displays and weapon-aiming avionics, or via his own IHADSS

An impressive quartet of daylight sensors; but the versatility of TADS does not end there. For night and adverse weather operations, the CP/G can switch to a 9in (23cm) FLIR, the optical port for which (and incidentally the largest-aperture unit of its type in tactical military service) dominates the left-hand portion of the TADS barrel-like turret.

Three fields-of-view (3.1deg, 10.1deg and 50deg) are available to the CP/G, and just as the DTV enables him to locate targets in conditions of visibility that would confound the DVO, so

Apache flight profiles

Below: The tactical situation dictates the combination of altitude and speed used in combat flight operations.

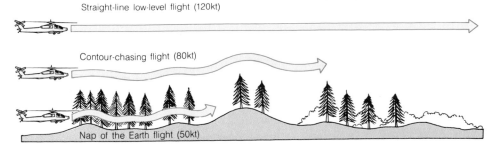

Straight-line low-level flight (120kt)

Contour-chasing flight (80kt)

Nap of the Earth flight (50kt)

The Eyes Have It

Hellfire indirect launch

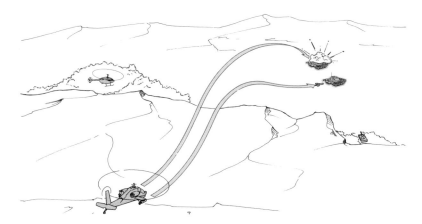

Above: Wherever possible, the Apache will try to stay out of the range of hostile air defences. Hellfire can be fired from a distance or behind cover at targets illuminated by other lasers. These designating lasers will be operated by light scout helicopters or ground observers, with the Apache out of sight.

the FLIR sensor can outperform the DTV to automatically track targets through smoke, dust etc. Built-in image intensifiers play a vital role in enabling the FLIR to cope with a significant degradation in weather conditions e.g. the absorption of much IR energy by water vapour present in the atmosphere.

This interchange extends to the use of the onboard sensors as well, with the DVO, DTV and FLIR the subject of a "mix and match" sensor infusion to create a three-dimensional effect through the integration of the human mind and the sensor systems. The results, in the form of crews with high kill rates, low probability of detection and excellent teamwork, speak for themselves.

But as formidable and versatile as the Apache's TADS/PNVS package is, there is always room for improvement. From the earliest days of the programme, sceptics cast doubt on the practicality of positioning the TADS/PNVS sensors in a low, nose-mounted turret, making it necessary for the Apache to reveal itself if a clear scan is to be achieved. Current US Army operational doctrine goes some way to negating this argument, with the 18 Apaches that typically constitute a Batallion supported by up to 13 Bell OH-58Ds, these trusty near-term scouts sporting prominent Mast-Mounted Sights (MMS) housing a x12 magnification TV camera, an auto-focusing IR thermal imaging sensor and LR/D, complete with automatic target tracking and in-flight automatic boresighting. Equally important, the OH-58D features an airborne target hand-off system.

The Apache itself is also the subject

Bottom: The optics built into the Bell OH-58D's mast-mounted sight enable this versatile helicopter to act as a forward scout for the Apache.

SECONDARY ROLE

Though TADS is principally operated by the CP/G, its wide-angle FLIR field-of-view and the high-quality video display provide an able night vision back-up should the PNVS fail. This versatility in operation has led to a significant degree of information interchange between pilot and CP/G, and the transfer of control if it is deemed necessary. Either man can spot the target, take charge, and by looking straight at the target through his IHADSS combiner glass, cue his partner and the available weapons to aim at the same spot.

Apache ambush

Above: In combat, Apaches will try to move forward to holding positions a few miles from the enemy. Once targets move onto the killing zone, the aircraft **move forward in NOE flight to the final launch positions. They then try to fire Hellfires in simultaneous salvos before preparing for the next ambush.**

of improvement and enhancement, the most ambitious project being the development of the Longbow Apache. Centred around a millimetre-wave (MM-W) radar and an upgraded version of the Hellfire (see Chapter Three), the Longbow Apache has the ability to track airborne or ground-based targets in conditions of adversity which defy the existing DTV and FLIR sensors. By adopting a mast-mounted location for the 300lb (136kg) MM-W radar, the Longbow Apache can track aerial targets through a complete 360deg, and ground targets through a highly impressive 270deg.

In addition, the system allows the Hellfire Optimized Missile System (HOMS), complete with its new Radio Frequency (RF) seeker head, to

Right: Immediately recognizeable by virtue of the 300lb (136kg) radar atop its main rotor, the Longbow Apache offers tremendous potential for enhanced fighting capabilities in the mid-1990s.

lock-on to the designated target at short ranges before the missile itself is launched. Alternatively, launches at longer-range targets can be enhanced by pre-programming the missile with target co-ordinates, thus allowing the missile to lock-on after its launch.

The US Army has budgeted for the modification of no less than 227 standad AH-64As to Longbow configuration. In truth, the service would have liked to convert more, if not all of its current Apache force, but even the figure of 227 may not be achieved by virtue of ever-tightening defence budgets.

At the time of writing, the first reports of the Apache's conduct in the Gulf War have filtered through. The 140 or so AH-64s were used to attack key troop installations in the front line in conjunction with the Air Force A-10 close-air support aircraft. Apaches fired the first shots of the air war when they destroyed a forward air defence radar with Hellfire missiles, minutes before the initial Allied air strikes crossed the border during the night of 16/17th January 1991 as the Allied air offensive swung into action.

"IT'S a great day to be at Fort Hood and in the Army." The words of Major General John Brown, Deputy Commander of the US Army's III Corps and Fort Hood, Texas, as he addressed a gathering of Army personnel and civilian dignitaries on 25 February 1986 in a ceremony to mark the arrival of the first quartet of AH-64A Apaches at the huge training base. The stage was set for the US Army's newest helicopter to enter service, and for crew training to begin in earnest.

Fort Hood had been chosen as the Apache's Unit Fielding Location as part of a novel Single-Station Unit Fielding and Training Plan, whereby all production Apaches would be delivered to the Texan base and issued to the units selected to convert onto the new machine with the help of the Apache Training Brigade (ATB).

However, the training programme at Fort Hood would concentrate on Battalion-level tuition; three other bases would be responsible for providing the specialized training of individuals in their respective roles, their programmes being co-ordinated and conducted under the auspices of the US Army's Training and Doctrine Command (TRADOC).

Located at Fort Eustis, Virginia, the Army Transportation and Aviation Logistics School (ATALS) was given the responsibility of familiarizing technicians and Maintenance Test Pilots (MTP) with the Apache's complex weapons and maintenance systems. Getting this training programme right from the outset was essetial, for the US Army had calculated that it would need some 900 fully-qualified maintenance personnel to graduate per year if the burgeoning

Above: Using the Apache's engine maintenance platform to its full effect, a groundcrew trainee gets "hands-on" work experience at Fort Eustis, Va., home of US Army maintenance training.

Apache fleet was to be properly maintained and operated.

To this end, 16 early-production AH-64As were assigned to ATALS, comprising ten Category-B (non-flyable) ground instruction trainers and six flyable machines. The latter examples would be used to support a 15-week MTP training programme.

At Fort Gordon, Georgia, home of the US Army's Signals School, a series of simulated airframes known as Integrated Avionics Maintenance Trainers (IAMT) were configured with comprehensive communication and navigation systems to facilitate tuition in working with the Apache's Automated Test Equipment (ATE) and avionics suite.

The third base involved in the

TRADOC programme was to be Fort Rucker, Alabama, where potential Apache aircrew would participate in the Aircrew Training Center's three-month Apache Qualification Course (AQC). Not surprisingly, a large force

Above: To facilitate transition from the AH-1 to the AH-64, a small number of the former have been fitted out with the nose-mounted PNVS sensor package.

Left: As the Apache training programme grew, so more of the new machines appeared on the various Aircrew Training Center flightlines within the confines of Fork Rucker, Ala.

of flight trainers was quickly established at the base, comprising 32 AH-64A Apaches and 10 unarmed, PNVS-equipped AH-1G Cobras transitional aircrew trainers.

Trainees would fly some 15 hours in the blacked out rear cockpit of the Cobra, as part of an 80-hour AQC flying programme. The balance of the AQC duration was to be given over to "ground school", and several high-tech, low-cost classroom training aids were put to good use to help instruct aircrew recruits in the Apache's flight procedures.

Above: One of several training tools used in Apache "ground school", the life-size CWEPT is used by the aircrew to hone their undoubted flying skills.

Top of the range is the highly impressive Combat Mission Simulator (CMS), complete with multiple, pre-programmed threat scenarios, and in which the pilots spend 18 gruelling hours' "flight time". Apart from providing uncannily realistic training scenarios, the CMS is also a highly economical training tool, with operating costs per hour approximately one-third those of the real Apache.

Computer-run Cockpit, Weapons and Emergency Procedures Trainers (CWEPT) are also important classroom training aids, permitting effective instruction in the Apache's numerous cockpit procedures. The back seat can be used as a Pilot-Selected Task Trainer (PSTT), while the TADS-Selected Task Trainer (TSTT) is used by CP/G trainees to familiarize themselves with the controls and firing procedures of the Apache's versatile weapons system.

GROUND SCHOOL

Numerically speaking, the most important ground-based training aids are the life-size Classroom System Trainers (CST) and the scaled-down version of the CST, known as Individual System Trainers (IST). Between them, these units cover virtually all of the Apache's systems, and give the trainee crewmen the chance to undertake highly realistic

but simulated "hands on" training in both systems operation procedures and troubleshooting.

Once the individual TRADOC training programmes have been completed at each of the three bases, the personnel come together as a team at Fort Hood, there to undergo a further three-stage, 90-day ATB training programme. Starting with 30 days' instruction at an individual level, the training continues with a Company-strength programme of like duration, and concludes with the Battalion training together as a single unit under front-line operational conditions.

Above: Slaved to computers on the outside, the CWEPT can provide the pilot and CP/G with highly realistic threat scenarios by way of computer-genrated images.

Warrior Charge

joined by the 1st and 2nd Battalions of the 6th Cavalry Regiment, 6th Cavalry Brigade (Air Combat). The qualification of these two units was particularly important, for though initially based at Fort Hood, they were soon to undertake a long and important overseas journey.

Flying south to Jefferson County Airport, just outside Beaumont, Texas, in August 1987, their Apaches were soon being ferried to the town dockyard, wrapped in protective plastic sheeting, and then loaded aboard two US Navy freighters. After some two weeks at sea, the ships arrived at their destination: Rotterdam, in the Netherlands.

A total of 127 US Army helicopters were offloaded from the USS *Algol*

The ATB programme concludes with an Army Readiness Training and Evaluation Programme (ARTEP) which, if completed successfully, will see the new Apache-equipped unit considered ready for deployment and active service. By the end of their ATB course, the unit will have accumulated in excess of 1,000 flying hours, as well as firing literally thousands of rounds of ammunition and ordnance.

During 1984/85, seven early-production Apaches were used at the manufacturer's Mesa-based Flight Test Center and at the US Army's Yuma Proving Grounds, with company test pilots training 37 Army pilots on the Apache. Known as the Initial Key Personnel Program (IKPT), the aim was to train and qualify an initial cadre of Instructor Pilots who would then pass on their knowledge to those selected to undergo type conversion.

Five of the 37-man IKPT cadre were Maintenance Test Pilots and they,

along with several of the early Apaches, were subsequently assigned to Fort Eustis to initiate the first Apache MTP training course, in November 1985.

A FIGHTING FORCE

Under the original Force Modernization Plan, the 7th Battalion of the 17th Cavalry Brigade (7/17th CAV) was to be the first of no less than 34 Army and Army National Guard (ARNG) Battalions to undergo Apache training. Of these, 24 would trade in their AH-1 Cobras, and 10 would be formed anew. By 1990, a total procurement of 612 production AH-64As was envisaged, with 18 examples assigned to each operating unit.

The 7/17th CAV completed its ARTEP at Fort Hood in April 1986, and over the next 18 months the Apache training programme gradually gathered pace. The first unit was soon

Above: Unceremoniously wrapped in protective plastic, an Apache is lowered into the hold of the USS *Algol* at Beaumont, Tx., as part of the build-up for *REFORGER '87*.

and USS *Capella* when they arrived at the Dutch port on 1 September and 8 September respectively, of which 38 were Apaches. Reassembled at dockside, they were subsequently ferried to Eindhoven for test-flying, and then onto what would be their operating area to the north of the German city of Hannover. The Apache was about to make its debut in Operation "*Certain Strike*", the name given to the transport, deployment and operation of US-based Army reinforcements alongside their NATO counterparts as part of *REFORGER '87* (REturn of FORces to GERmany).

During the following weeks, the 1/6th CAV and 2/6th CAV Apaches flew some 725 mission hours, mostly at night and often in the adverse weather conditions so typical of Europe. Ably supported by their groundcrew teams, the units posted a combined mission-capable rate of over

Below: The warrior and his trusty scout, namely the Bell OH-58D as used by USAREUR units to probe enemy lines prior to the Apache coming in to make the kill.

90 per cent, and more than proved the Apache's fighting abilities.

That the Apache's experiences during *REFORGER '87* were in the main positive was significant, for the US Army's fielding programme called for the first active US Army in Europe (USAREUR) Apache unit to be operationally capable by January 1988. In addition, no less than 14 of the 34 units scheduled to acquire the Apache would subsequently be assigned to USAREUR.

Following the conclusion of the exercise, the 2/6th CAV remained in-country and deployed to its new German home at Immelsheim. Meanwhile, the 1/6th CAV returned to Fort Hood, where the training of further units was continuing apace.

ON GUARD

In October 1987, another Apache "first" was achieved when a 36-man cadre from the 30th Attack Helicopter Battalion of the North Carolina Army National Guard (NC ARNG) completed its training programme, and returned to Raleigh-Durham Airport to instruct fellow Guardsmen. In due

course, the unit would be joined by a South Carolina-based ARNG Battalion, and both would mobilize with the 1st Battalion of the 82nd Aviation Regiment, 82nd Airborne Division, based at Fort Bragg, NC. The 1/82nd AVN became the sixth unit to convert to the Apache, following the "graduation" of the 5/17th CAV (subsequently redesignated the 1/3rd AVN) and the 1/227th AVN in August and October 1987 respectively.

The list of Apache-equipped units grew during 1988 to include the 5/6th CAV and the 4/229th AVN, both of which would commence deployment to the West German bases of Wiesbaden and Immelsheim during the second half of the year as the second and third USAREUR Apache-equipped Battalions respectively.

As previously mentioned, the US Army's original force deployment plan envisaged a German-based Apache force numbering 14 Battalions, equipped with a total of 252 Apaches. The subsequent deployment of the 3/1st AVN and 3/227th AVN to Ansbach and Hanau as the decade drew to a close meant that by the time USAREUR forces prepared for

Warrior Charge

US ARMY PROCUREMENT

First Production Contract placed on 15th April 1982. Known as Lot 1, it covered a total of 11 AH-64As (PV-01 to PV-10) and was funded as part of the FY82 US Defense Budget.

Initial plans called for a 475-strong Apache fleet, although this figure was to fluctuate considerably. Current plans call for a total of 807 AH-64As.

Production is covered in Lots 1-10 (FY82 to FY91), with the 807th and final AH-64A for the US Army due to be completed in 1993.

REFORGER '89, just over one-third of the Apache force was in place, with a further three units scheduled to deploy to German bases during the early-1990s.

FORCE REDUCTIONS

However, any real chances of USAREUR ever actually fielding all 14 Apache units are extremely remote, for the rapid thaw in Cold War superpower relations has all but negated the awesome threat once posed by some 56,000 WarPac tanks, poised to cut through NATO front-line defences and sweep westward through Germany. Not surprisingly, the wholesale reduction and even elimination of the weapons of war — especially the tank and AFV forces — is now the most obvious manifestation of the so-called "Peace Dividend", with the result that the need for a large USAREUR anti-armour attack helicopter force has been effectively discredited.

The US Army's anti-armour capabilities are but one aspect of an across-the-board re-evaluation of US defence priorities, in both quantitative and qualitative terms. A general downsizing of the US armed forces and a fundamental reassessment of their operational roles and requirements is now the order of the day, coupled with deep cuts in the finance available to support current and future weapons acquisition programmes.

The Apache has not escaped the planned cuts, and the powers-that-be on Capitol Hill have decided that procurement funding will cease at a total of 807 AH-64As; a far cry from the heady days when MDDH Army and leaders talked confidentaly of production figures well in excess of 1,000, and a decision that has inevitably led MDDH to announce sizeable reductions in production personnel.

Vested interests apart, the fact that the likelihood of front-line Apaches going into combat to counter the push of WarPac armour forces is now viewed as most unlikely is, of course, something for which the world can be thankful. Elsewhere, however, the general warming in East-West relations has had little effect, and though it may never fire in anger over Northern Europe, the Apache has still managed to pick up a few "scalps" in recent times, albeit in wholly different combat scenarios and far away from the plains of Northern Europe.

The Apache's combat debut came in December 1989, when US forces launched Operation "*Just Cause*" in Panama, in an attempt to remove the dictator General Manuel Noriega from power. The operation was primarily a US Army action, with airborne support provided by some 170 helicopters grouped in Task Force *Aviation*, including eleven 1/82nd AVN Apaches delivered in-country by C-5 transports.

INTO BATTLE

At 00:45am on 20 December, the US forces attacked with the aim of removing Noriega and the Panamanian Defence Force from power, protecting the Panama Canal, and installing a democratically-elected government. The Apaches (operating under the auspices of Task Force *Wolf*) were in the thick of the fighting from the outset of hostilities, and between 20 December 1989 and 9 January 1990, they flew 247 combat hours. During an attack on Noriega's headquarters, Hellfire missiles were fired into the building through individual windows from a distance of 2 miles (4km); and

Below: Apaches can be easily transported by C-5 Galaxy. The items coloured pink are detached, the items coloured blue are stowed.

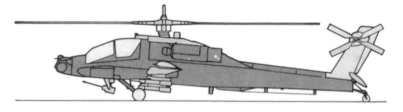

further successes included the destruction of two V-300 Armoured Personnel Carriers, again courtesy of Hellfires.

In addition to overt attack operations, full use was made of the Apache's night vision capabilities to conduct effective night-time armed reconnaissance sorties, directing US ground forces as they progressed through Panama City building by building, block by block.

The Apache's contribution to Operation "*Just Cause*" was deemed a success by the US Army; but the armchair critics back in the United States were soon highlighting combat shortcomings. Certainly there were some operational mishaps. One machine was grounded through hydraulic failure just prior to the launch of the assault, and its replacement subsequently suffered a loss of TADS imagery when vibration from the M230 Chain Gun during firing inadvertantly popped a circuit breaker. A third Apache had its Chain Gun

Right: The value of the Apache's ability to be airlifted six at a time by the C-5 Galaxy was fully underscored during the recent Gulf War, when over 140 Apaches were delivered in-theatre.

Left: Disappearing into the vast, gaping "mouth" of a US Air Force C-5A Galaxy, an Apache with its wings "clipped" is readied for air transport.

jammed when a Panamanian bullet lodged in the feed mechanism.

However, these experiences must be put into perspective. All of the damaged machines managed to return to base, and all were flying again after overnight maintenance and repair work. Overall, the eleven Apaches posted an 81 per cent mission-capable rate; and the ability to absorb and survive defensive fire was ably demonstrated when one machine took no less than 23 hits from small-arms fire. Despite damage to a gearbox, tail rotor drive-shaft and the main rotor blades, the Apache was successfully nursed back home to base.

There can be no doubt that the profiles of the missions conducted by the Apaches over Panama were far removed from those tank-busting scenarios previously envisaged by US Army commanders. Yet at the time of writing, the possibility of Apaches being used in anger in their primary anti-armour role is a very real

possibility. This time, the deserts of the Gulf region form the backdrop, as Operation "Desert Shield" pits US air, land and sea forces against Iraq in defence of oil-rich Saudi Arabia.

"DESERT STORM"

Just how the Gulf crisis is finally resolved remains to be seen, as does the impact on future US defence spending, but it is conceivable that the Apache, like several other weapon systems, could benefit from revised defence priorities as a result of US military experience during "*Desert Shield*". What is far more certain is that MDDH will benefit in the form of increased export orders, most notably from pro-Western Gulf states vulnerable to attack from their larger, more aggressive neighbours.

Unless US procurement plans are revised, production of the last Apache for the US Army is scheduled for 1993, even allowing for a reduced production rate of six-per-month. Not surprisingly, MDDH has redoubled its efforts to sell the Apache abroad, although like any good manufacturer with faith in its product, the company has put considerable effort into winn-

ing export sales since the early days of the Apache production programme. Yet it is only recently that such efforts have borne fruit.

There is more than a little irony in the fact that both the first and second export customers — Israel and Egypt — have more than a passing interest in events in the Gulf. A long-time recipient of military aid from the United States, the Israeli Defence Force/Air Force (IDF/AF) is set to receive 18 AH-64As, the first of which was delivered in late-1990. Full support and training is included in the deal, as they are in the agreement concluded with Egypt covering 24 AH-64As.

ARAB ORDERS

Moving south-east, MDDH is set to find further export success as a direct result of current tensions in the Gulf. Jolted by the actions of Iraq and the threat posed to its neighbour, Saudi Arabia, the United Arab Emirates (UAE) announced in September 1990 its plans to procure 18 AH-64As.

An order for up to three times the number ordered by the UAE has been mentioned in connection with the West's closest ally in the region — Saudi Arabia itself. With Iraqi forces stationed to the north and in Kuwait, and with the massed arsenal of the multi-national defence force on its soil, it is hardly surprising that the Saudis are set to embark on a potentially huge military spending spree, part of which will cover the acquisition of Apaches.

Several other nations have been mentioned as potential Apache customers, including the Japanese Ground Self-Defence Force (JGSDF). Currently operating 70+ AH-1S's, the JGSDF has intimated that it may acquire a small number of Apaches in the mid-1990s for operational trials; but unit costs and increasing pressure to reduce defence expenditure may put paid to any such plans.

A far more likely market for MDDH is Europe, specifically the armies of the Netherlands and Great Britain. Given that the Apache was built first and foremost as an anti-tank asset for NATO forces facing the threat of the Warsaw Pact, the lack of sales to date within the ranks of NATO is somewhat surprising.

For the Netherlands, the need to replace its ageing Alouette IIIs has led to interest in the Apache, with a potential requirement for up to 50 such machines. There is a strong possibility, however, that any Apaches procured for the Dutch Army would be the subject of a leasing agreement with the US Army, rather than an outright purchase from MDDH. It is also more than likely that any such acquisition will involve a smaller number of machines, possibly around 20-24.

APACHE v TIGER

A far more likely customer, and potentially a far bigger prize for MDDH, is Great Britain's Army Air Corps (AAC), which established a need for a next-generation attack helicopter to replace its Westland Lynx force during the 1990s as long ago as 1984. Participation in the ill-fated Tonal programme (along with the Netherlands, Italy and Spain) was terminated during 1990, leaving two contenders for an order of at least 50-75 machines: the Eurocopter Tiger and the MDDH Apache.

The former is arguably a more advanced weapons system — or rather it will be, for the Tiger has yet to fly. Nevertheless, there is strong political pressure on Great Britain to toe the European line and place its faith in the Tiger, even though such participation would likely be as very much the junior production partner.

The Apache, on the other hand, is openly favoured by the AAC, and is attractive to the politicians in that the standard system could be bought ''off the shelf'', thus saving both time and money. Whether this will happen in reality is open to question, for current talk is of the majority — or maybe all — of any AAC order comprising Longbow Apaches (this variant having been approved for sale to Great

Left: Seen here in its full-scale mock-up form, the Franco-German Eurocopter Tiger is chief rival to the Apache when it comes to potential European orders.

Above: Following up on potential interest in a maritime version, MDDH released this impression of the Sea Apache, complete with a prominent rotor-mounted radar.

Britain by the US Department of Defense in August 1990), and with British avionics, such as the GEC-Marconi *Brimstone* millimetre-wave guidance system, carried onboard.

MARITIME MARKET

While any such sales, real or imagined, are based around the AH-64A and Longbow variants designed primarily to meet the air-land battle needs, brief mention should be made of a navalized variant — the Sea Apache — which has been touted as a potential combat asset for both the US Navy (USN) and the US Marine Corps (USMC).

As early as September 1981, a YAH-64 was evaluated with a view to establishing the Apache's suitability for operations from the decks of amphibious vessels. Proponents of the so-called Sea Apache envisaged USMC machines flying shotgun for troop-carrying CH-46 Sea Knight and CH-53 Sea Stallion transport helicopters, toting AAMs, FFARs and the Chain Gun to counter both ground and air opposition.

For the US Navy, a more traditional seaborne helicopter role was envisaged, with Sea Apaches undertaking anti-ship and air-defence missions, as well as providing anti-ship surveillance and targeting (ASTT) back-up for the Sikorsky SH-60B Seahawk force.

The first artistic impressions of a navalized Apache showed the familiar angular lines, but with the US Army's dark green camouflage having given way to a cloak of light grey. There were also some notable additions to onboard systems, including a rotor head-mounted radar and a mix of air-to-air and air-to-surface missiles.

In 1987, MDDH issued a revised artistic impression of the Sea Apache, the most obvious difference being the deletion of the TADS/PNVS suite and Chain Gun to make way for a completely new, smooth-contoured nose radome, this to house an APG-65 multi-mode search radar. Additional features included retractable main landing gear units, mounted outrigger style to increase the helicopter's stability when operating from pitching and rolling decks, and an increased fuel capacity to enable missions of up to 6 hours' duration. Endurance could be further extended via an in-flight refuelling probe located on the starboard side of the new nose.

During its time in the limelight, the talk was of nearly 100 Sea Apaches being required by the USN, these to be divided amongst four squadrons with sea-going detachments. In reality, however, both the USN and USMC proposals have remained on the drawing board, with ever-diminishing chances of either service having the necessary funds to enable further proof-of-concept evaluation.

Below: A radically-altered view of the Sea Apache was released in 1987, with a completely new nose radome covering a Hughes APG-65 multi-mode search radar.

INDEX